MY PET
GUINEA PIG

Jill Foran

W
Weigl Publishers Inc.

Published by Weigl Publishers Inc.
350 5th Avenue, Suite 3304, PMB 6G
New York, NY 10118-0069
Web site: www.weigl.com

Project Coordinator
Heather C. Hudak

Design and Layout
Terry Paulhus

Library of Congress Cataloging-in-Publication Data

Foran, Jill.
 Guinea pig / Jill Foran.
     p. cm. -- (My pet)
 Includes index.
 ISBN 978-1-60596-090-6 (hard cover : alk. paper) -- ISBN 978-1-60596-091-3 (soft
 cover : alk. paper)
 1. Guinea pig--Juvenile literature. I. Title.
 SF401.G85F67 2010
 636.935'92--dc22
                                    2009005128

Printed in China
1 2 3 4 5 6 7 8 9 0   13 12 11 10 09

Photograph and Text Credits

Every reasonable effort has been made to trace ownership and to obtain
permission to reprint copyright material. The publishers would be pleased
to have any errors or omissions brought to their attention so that they may
be corrected in subsequent printings.

All of the Internet URLs given in the book were valid at the time of publication.
However, due to the dynamic nature of the Internet, some addresses may have
changed, or sites may have ceased to exist since publication. While the author
and publisher regret any inconvenience this may cause readers, no responsibility
for any such changes can be accepted by either the author or the publisher.

Weigl acknowledges Getty Images as its primary image supplier for this title.

Diane Calkins/Click the Photo Connection: page 7 bottom left, 7 bottom right;
Gerry Bucsis & Barbara Somerville: pages 6 left, 7 top right.

Contents

4 Guinea Pig Pals

6 Pet Profiles

8 Crazy for Cavies

10 Life Cycle

12 Picking Your Pet

14 Guinea Pig Gear

16 Guinea Pigging Out

18 From Feet to Fur

20 Keeping Clean

22 Healthy and Happy

24 Cavy Comfort

26 Best in Show

28 Pet Puzzlers

30 Frequently Asked Questions

31 More Information

32 Words to Know and Index

Guinea Pig Pals

Guinea pigs make great pets. Their cute faces, pudgy bodies, and gentle nature have made them popular household companions in many parts of the world. Not only are guinea pigs cute, they are easy to care for. They are clean and quiet, and do not require much space. Guinea pigs have very good **temperaments.**

Guinea pigs are very fragile and must not be dropped. If your guinea pig begins to squirm when you are holding him, put him down right away.

Although guinea pigs are good natured, looking after them is a big responsibility. Once you have a pet guinea pig, you must take care of him every day. You must give him what he needs to live a happy and healthy life. Guinea pigs require a balanced diet, plenty of exercise, and plenty of attention. If you give your pet the love and care he needs, he will return your love.

Porky Pig

- Another name for a guinea pig is cavy. The name cavy comes from the scientific term *Cavia porcellus*. Guinea pigs belong to the Cavia porcellus species.
- Guinea pigs are not related to pigs. They belong to a group of animals called rodents, which also includes chinchillas, gerbils, hamsters, mice, porcupines, and rats.

Pet Profiles

There are thirteen **breeds** of **domestic** guinea pig. There are even more crossbreeds. Crossbreed guinea pigs are born to parents that are of two or more different breeds. Purebred guinea pigs have parents of the same breed. Knowing the different types of guinea pigs will help you to choose your perfect pet.

Guinea pigs come in a variety of colors. Those that have coats of one color are called self types. Non-self, or marked, types can have up to three colors in their coats. Aside from different coat colors, guinea pigs also have different hairstyles. Some have hair that is long and silky. Others have short, wiry coats. Some even have hair that grows in **tufts** all over their bodies.

abyssinian

- Short, wiry coat
- Hair grows in spiral tufts called rosettes
- Most have five to ten rosettes
- Ridge along the spine
- Does not like to be handled as much as smooth-haired guinea pigs
- Mustache around the nose

american

- Most popular breed for pet owners
- Short, smooth coat
- Easy to **groom**
- Grows to be 10 to 14 inches (25 to 36 centimeters) in length
- Also known as the English Cavy

PERUVIAN

- Long, smooth coat
- Hair parts down the middle of the back and grows over the sides, rump, head, and face
- Needs to be groomed quite often
- Hair grows up to 20 inches (51 cm) long

TEDDY

- Popular pet in the United States
- Short, dense coat that sticks out from the body
- Fur bounces back up when patted down
- Easy to groom
- Large, bright eyes

SILKIE

- Long, silky coat that grows 8 to 10 inches (20 to 25 cm) long
- Head and face are not covered with hair
- Also known as a sheltie
- Baby silkies look like American guinea pigs

WHITE CRESTED

- Short, smooth coat
- Single, white rosette on top of the head
- Large, bold eyes
- Roman nose, which is a nose that is higher than normal at the top

Crazy for Cavies

Guinea pigs come from South America, where they have lived in the wild for thousands of years. South American Native Peoples called Incas were **taming** and breeding wild guinea pigs as early as 9000 BC. In the 1500s, European sailors began arriving in South America. Some of these sailors took guinea pigs back home to Europe. Soon, people in many parts of Europe wanted to keep guinea pigs as pets.

Do not put any plastic items in your guinea pig's hutch. Your pet may chew the plastic and swallow pieces she cannot digest.

At first, guinea pigs were very expensive. Only rich people or royalty could afford to buy these furry friends. However, as time passed, guinea pigs became more affordable. When Europeans began to settle in North America, they brought their pet guinea pigs with them.

It is not known where the name guinea pig came from. Guinea pigs do not come from Guinea, Africa, and they do not look like pigs. Some people believe that guinea pigs were given the guinea part of their name by Spanish sailors. The sailors sold guinea pigs for one gold coin, known as a guinea. Stories also say that the animals were given the pig part of their name because they squeal like pigs.

Cavy Crazy

- Wild cavies still live in the grasslands and mountains of South America. As many as 10 wild cavies live together in burrows, or underground homes. They search for food at night.
- If a wild guinea pig is being chased by a **predator**, she might pretend to be dead.

Life Cycle

Guinea pigs have a life span of 5 to 8 years. With proper care, some guinea pigs can live even longer. A guinea pig has different needs at different stages of his life. At all stages of life, a guinea pig will depend on his owner for love and attention.

Newborn Guinea Pigs

Newborn guinea pigs are called puppies. Unlike newborn hamsters or rabbits, puppies have fur. In fact, they look like smaller versions of their parents. Puppies are born with their eyes open and have a full set of teeth. Within a few days, puppies are able to walk and nibble food.

Three to Five Weeks

Guinea pigs stop drinking their mother's milk when they are about 3 weeks old. They are very playful and curious. Young guinea pigs can have babies. However, they are too young to make good parents. To prevent young guinea pigs from mating, the males and females should be kept apart.

Adulthood

By 5 or 6 months of age, guinea pigs are fully grown. Both male and female guinea pigs are now mature enough to take care of babies. Adult guinea pigs are active and social. They like to be kept busy. For example, guinea pigs like to play with old socks, shoe boxes, tennis balls, and plumbing pipes.

Mature Guinea Pigs

Guinea pigs mature at different times. As guinea pigs start to age, their coats become dull, and they begin to lose hair. Mature guinea pigs will sleep more and play less. Guinea pigs that have reached maturity are more likely to develop illnesses.

Living Life

- A mother guinea pig is pregnant for about 70 days. This is a long time compared to other rodents.
- In nature, guinea pigs are born in the open, with little to protect them from danger. Puppies need to be quite developed at birth so they can protect themselves against predators.

11

Picking Your Pet

Choosing a guinea pig is a big responsibility. There are many things to consider before selecting a new pet. The following questions will help you to decide what type of guinea pig is right for you.

Try to choose a guinea pig that is about 6 weeks old. Young guinea pigs are easier to tame.

Which Type of Guinea Pig Should I Get?

All guinea pigs, no matter what their breed, are friendly and easy to handle. Probably the most important thing to consider when choosing a pet is how much time you want to spend grooming his coat. Breeds with smooth, short coats are the easiest to keep clean and well groomed. Longhaired guinea pigs, such as Peruvians or silkies, need much more time and attention. Their long coats require brushing and cleaning every day, and their fur must be trimmed quite often.

Where Can I Buy a Pet Guinea Pig?

The most common place to buy a guinea pig is a pet store. Pet stores usually sell crossbred guinea pigs. If you want to purchase a purebred guinea pig, you will probably have to go to a private **breeder**. Breeders know much about the guinea pigs they raise. They will be able to provide information and tips about how to care for your new pet. You may also be able to get a guinea pig at a local animal shelter. Often, animal shelters have many older guinea pigs in need of good homes.

What Should I Look for When I Am Picking My Guinea Pig?

Try to choose a guinea pig that is in good health. A healthy guinea pig should be plump. His coat should be shiny and free of bald spots. He should be alert and curious, and his eyes should be bright and clear. His nose should be dry, and his ears should be clean.

Name Calling

- A male guinea pig is called a boar, and a female guinea pig is called a sow.

- An average sow weighs about 2 pounds (0.5 kilogram). Boars weigh slightly more than sows.

Guinea Pig Gear

Moving to a new home can be stressful for any animal. To help make your guinea pig feel more comfortable, it is a good idea to be prepared with some basic equipment. The most important item your new pet will need is a cage or a hutch. Most pet stores sell large guinea pig cages. However, many people believe that a wooden hutch is a better house for a guinea pig. A wooden hutch usually has more space than a wire cage. Whatever kind of house you choose, make sure that it has proper **ventilation** and a solid bottom. It should also have separate areas for playing and sleeping.

Do not put cedar wood shavings inside your pet's cage. Cedar is toxic to guinea pigs.

Your pet guinea pig will settle nicely into his new home if you make the space as comfortable as possible. The floor of the hutch should be covered with **absorbent** wood shavings. Your pet can burrow in these shavings. Be sure to provide your guinea pig with plenty of bedding material, too. Wood shavings, hay, and straw can be used for bedding. The hutch should also have a large water bottle, a piece of wood for **gnawing**, and a food bowl that will not tip over.

Warm Blooded

- Guinea pigs are happiest and healthiest in places where the temperature is above 65 degrees Fahrenheit (18 degrees Celsius).
- Guinea pigs can be trained to use a litter box.

Guinea Pigging Out

Guinea pigs are herbivores, which means that they only eat plant matter. There is no meat in their diets. The best way to ensure that your pet guinea pig is getting the proper **nutrition** is to give her guinea pig feed pellets. These pellets are available at most pet stores and at many supermarkets. Your guinea pig should also be given fresh fruits and vegetables every day, as well as plenty of hay.

Leftover fruits and vegetables can rot if they are not removed from the cage each day.

It is important to feed your guinea pig twice a day. Try to feed your pet at the same time each day. Guinea pigs are creatures of habit. They like a set routine, and they look forward to their mealtimes.

When you first get your guinea pig, ask a **veterinarian** or a breeder how much food to give your pet. Be sure to provide your guinea pig with a constant supply of water, too. A guinea pig should never be without fresh, clean water.

fresh Squeezed

- Just like humans, guinea pigs are unable to produce vitamin C in their own bodies. Without enough vitamin C, guinea pigs are likely to develop an illness called **scurvy**.

To prevent scurvy, be sure to give your pet fresh foods that are rich in vitamin C, including broccoli, carrots, cauliflower, and oranges.

From Feet to Fur

Although guinea pig types look different, they have many of the same features. All guinea pigs have similar sizes and weights. They all have plump, round bodies, short tails, and fragile skeletons. They also have thick necks to support their large heads. Guinea pigs have large stomachs that allow them to digest their **vegetarian** meals easily. They also have short legs so that they never have to crouch down far to pick up food.

Guinea pigs have twenty teeth. Their teeth are open-rooted, which means that they never stop growing. Guinea pigs use their sharp front teeth to bite and gnaw their food.

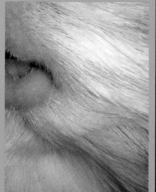

Guinea pigs have large, glossy eyes located on the sides of their head. Guinea pigs can see colors. They are also able to see more images per second than humans. A guinea pig sees 33 images per second, while a human sees an average of 20 images per second.

Guinea pigs have three toes on their back feet and four toes on their front feet. Each foot has sharp claws and leathery soles, or pads, that cover the bottom. These pads help protect the animal's fragile toe bones.

Guinea pigs have a good sense of hearing. They can hear high-pitched sounds much better than humans. Most guinea pigs are able to recognize other guinea pigs by the sounds they make.

Guinea pigs have a keen sense of smell. They use their little pink noses to sniff out danger.

The whiskers on a guinea pig's face are quite long, like a cat's whiskers. Guinea pigs use their whiskers to find objects in the dark.

Keeping Clean

Guinea pigs are very clean animals. They are happiest when their home is neat and tidy. To help keep a guinea pig happy and healthy, the owner should clean his cage daily. When cleaning a guinea pig's cage, droppings and soiled bedding should be removed, and the feeding equipment should be washed. Remember to put fresh bedding, food, and water in the cage.

Use a soft baby brush or a toothbrush when grooming your guinea pig. Brushes with harder bristles may scratch and harm your pet's skin.

Your guinea pig's home will need a more thorough cleaning once a week. To do this, take everything out of the cage, and scrub it with hot, soapy water or a mild cleanser that is safe for animals. Make sure the cage is rinsed well and completely dry before putting in fresh shavings and bedding.

Guinea pigs also like to look their best. Most guinea pigs groom themselves regularly. They use their front paws and teeth as combs and their tongue as a washcloth. Although most guinea pigs keep themselves clean, owners should help with their grooming. Smooth-haired breeds should be brushed once a week. Breeds with rough or long coats need to be brushed and combed every day.

Claw Clipping

- Guinea pigs file their teeth by gnawing on wood. Always be sure to have a piece of gnawing wood in your pet's cage. If your guinea pig's teeth are too long or uneven, a veterinarian will have to clip them. A veterinarian can also clip your pet's claws.

Healthy and Happy

Guinea pigs are usually healthy animals. If they receive proper care, they rarely become ill. To keep your guinea pig in top shape, feed her a balanced diet. You need to groom her and clean out her hutch regularly, too. Guinea pigs are nervous pets, and they scare easily. This can be harmful to their health. Loud noises and too much handling are common sources of stress for guinea pigs.

Examine your pet's coat every day to make sure it is free of lice and mites.

To avoid scaring your pet, always speak softly, and do not let too many people handle her. Keep her hutch in a quiet place where she will not be frightened by sudden noises or other pets.

Sometimes, even if a guinea pig is given proper care, she may become ill. Whenever you are handling your guinea pig, give her a quick health check. Your guinea pig might be sick if she is eating less food, exercising less often, or has wetness around her eyes and nose. If you notice any of these **symptoms**, take your guinea pig to a veterinarian right away.

Climate Control

- Guinea pigs can catch colds from drafts, dampness, or temperature changes.
- Guinea pigs need to exercise. Many owners let their guinea pigs run free in the house or garden. Owners must be sure to watch their guinea pig closely when she is outdoors. Others build an exercise run, which is a long cage that can be placed on the floor or on the ground outside.

Cavy Comfort

When owners first bring their guinea pig home, he will probably be nervous and shy. New owners may want to play with their new pet right away. It is best to leave him alone for a while. Quietly watch your guinea pig as he explores and settles into his hutch.

Be sure to keep your pet's cage away from the television or stereo. Loud noises scare guinea pigs.

After a day or two, spend some time talking softly to your pet so he will get to know your voice. Let another day pass before offering your guinea pig food from your hand. Once he is comfortable being fed by hand, you can try to hold him.

When you are ready to pick up your guinea pig, approach him from the front so he is able to see you coming. Move slowly to avoid startling him. Pick up your guinea pig gently, placing one hand around his shoulders and the other under his bottom. Hold your pet for a short time at first. Each day, slowly increase the amount of time you spend handling your guinea pig. After a while, your guinea pig will be happy to see you approaching.

Pet Peeves
Guinea pigs do not like:

- loud noises
- having their fur ruffled
- too much attention
- too little attention
- being too hot or too cold
- straw bedding instead of hay

Call of the Wild

- Guinea pigs enjoy using their voices. When they are content, they make a variety of noises, including gurgles, grunts, and squeaks.

- On occasion, you may see your guinea pig jump high into the air. This jumping is called "popcorning," and it is the sign of a happy, healthy guinea pig.

Best in Show

Humans have been raising and breeding guinea pigs for thousands of years. At first, early South Americans tamed wild guinea pigs to use as a source of food.

Guinea Pig Tales

In *Jenius: The Amazing Guinea Pig*, Judy has two pet guinea pigs named Molly and Joe. One day, Molly gives birth to a baby guinea pig. Judy names the baby Jenius. Jenius is a very smart guinea pig. He can perform many tricks, such as sit, stay, and play dead. Judy wants to prove that guinea pigs are smarter than people think. She takes Jenius to school for show-and-tell, but he does not perform his tricks. Now, Judy must find another way to prove Jenius has talent.
From Dave King-Smith's *Jenius: The Amazing Guinea Pig*.

As time passed, people all over the world began to realize that guinea pigs made better pets than meals. Today, guinea pigs are very popular animals. Not only are they kept as pets, some have even appeared in films and television shows. One of the best-known cavy stars is GP the Guinea Pig. He is the clever inventor on the television show *Hammy the Hamster*.

A popular hobby for many guinea pig owners is entering their pets into shows. Cavy shows and competitions are held all over the world. Prizes are given to the best guinea pig handler at these competitions. The judges follow a set of guidelines, or rules, that help them select a winner. If you wish to show your pet, join a local cavy club and attend as many shows as possible.

Space Cadets

- Guinea pigs can be taught tricks. With the right treats and plenty of patience, you can teach your guinea pig to waltz, jump, and turn in a circle.

- Guinea pigs were among the first small **mammals** to be sent to outer space.

Pet Puzzlers

How much do you know about guinea pigs? If you can answer the following questions correctly, you may be ready to own a pet guinea pig.

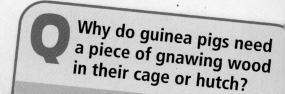

Q Why do guinea pigs need a piece of gnawing wood in their cage or hutch?

A Guinea pigs use gnawing wood to file their front teeth.

Q How often should a guinea pig be fed?

A Most veterinarians say that a pet guinea pig should be fed twice each day. If possible, owners should also try to feed their pet at the same time each day.

Q How many years do guinea pigs live?

A Guinea pigs usually live to be 5 to 8 years old.

Q How often should guinea pigs be groomed?

A A smooth-haired guinea pig should be groomed once a week. A rough or longhaired guinea pig should be groomed every day.

Q What is popcorning?

A Popcorning is the term used to describe when a guinea pig jumps high in the air. Popcorning is a sign of a happy guinea pig.

Q Do guinea pigs see in black and white or in color?

A Guinea pigs see in color. They especially like the color green.

Q What are some signs that a guinea pig is sick?

A A guinea pig might be sick if she is eating less food, exercising less often, or has wetness around her eyes and nose.

Calling Your Cavy

Before you buy your pet guinea pig, write down some guinea pig names that you like. Some names may work better for a female guinea pig. Others may suit a male guinea pig. Here are just a few suggestions.

Popcorn

Trixie

Ginger

Porky

Arnold

Barney

Patches

Rex

Lucy

Lady

Should I get more than one guinea pig?

Guinea pigs are very social animals. In nature, they live in groups of five to ten. Pet guinea pigs are happiest and healthiest when they have at least one cavy companion. If you decide to keep only one guinea pig as a pet, be sure to give him plenty of attention.

Should I breed my guinea pigs?

Breeding guinea pigs is a big responsibility. You should think carefully before putting a male and a female together. A female guinea pig can have a litter of four puppies. The mother will care for her puppies for the first few weeks following their births. After that, it will be your responsibility to care for the young guinea pigs.

Should I keep my guinea pig's hutch inside or outside?

If you live in a mild climate, you can let your guinea pig live outside for most of the year. Be sure to position the hutch in a place that is protected from direct sunlight, drafts, and bad weather. The hutch should be raised off the ground, and it should have strong door latches. This will help keep your guinea pig from getting out, and it will keep other animals from getting in. Guinea pigs do not like weather that is too cold or too hot. When the weather gets too extreme, be sure to bring your pet inside.

More Information

Animal Organizations

You can help guinea pigs stay happy and healthy by learning more about them. Many organizations are dedicated to teaching people how to care for and protect their pet pals. For more guinea pig information, write to the following organizations.

Golden State Cavy Breeders Association

718 Newburgh Court
Fairfield, CA 94533

American Rabbit Breeders Association

8 Westport Court
Bloomington, IL 61704

Websites

To answer more of your guinea pig questions, go online, and surf to the following websites.

Guinea Pigs Club

www.guineapigsclub.com

Guinea Pig Fun

www.guineapigfun.com

Cavy Madness

www.cavymadness.com

Words to Know

absorbent: able to soak up moisture

breeder: a person who raises specific types of animals or plants

breeds: groups of animals that share certain characteristics

domestic: tamed and used to living among people; not living in the wild

gnawing: wearing away by nonstop biting or chewing

groom: cleaning by removing dirt and tangles from fur

mammals: warm-blooded animals that have hair and drink their mother's milk

nutrition: the proper food needed for health

predator: an animal that hunts and kills other animals for food

scurvy: a disease that causes loose teeth, bruises, bleeding gums, and muscle pain

symptoms: signs of illness

taming: to change from living in the wild to living among people

temperaments: personalities

tufts: clumps or clusters

vegetarian: an animal that does not eat meat or fish

ventilation: constant fresh air

veterinarian: animal doctor

Abyssinian guinea pig 6
American guinea pig 6, 7

bedding 15, 21, 25
breeds 6, 13, 21

cage 14, 16, 20, 21, 23, 24, 28
cavy 5, 6, 8, 9, 24, 27, 29, 30, 31
cleaning 13, 21

food 9, 10, 15, 17, 18, 19, 20, 23, 25, 26, 29

grooming 6, 7, 13, 20, 21, 22, 29

handling 6, 22, 23, 25
health 5, 13, 22, 23, 25, 30, 31
hutch 14, 15, 22, 23, 24, 28, 30

life cycle 10, 11

Peruvian guinea pig 6, 13
pet peeves 25

silkie guinea pig 7, 13
South America 8, 9

teddy guinea pig 7

veterinarian 17, 21, 23, 28

white crested guinea pig 7